One Night of Seduction
by Iisha Taylor

For permission requests, write to the publisher at:
Iisha Taylor

Ashi Publishing
LuvHerGirlWorld.press@gmail.com

ISBN: 979-8-9951456-0-8

Printed in the United States

To all my lovers who still believe in love, know that love truly does exist, and that is evident because of who you are.

Table of Contents

Table of Contents

Table of Contents

Fine Wine

Fine wine over here!
You can pour me into a glass,
swirl me around
and take hits of all my notes.
And over time,
only those with taste
will be able to indulge.

Feel Me

SWEETHEART,
at the end of the day,
I just want you to feel something.
If only you can you feel me?

Monitor

Working to keep my energy aligned,
with something I can get behind,
a major role player
that doesn't have to say every line.

Let's Link

I want inappropriate conversations
with some healthy food,
to balance out what comes in and out of our mouths.
And if I get the chance to put my mouth on
you, the good and bad I'd do.

See, I need not talk much,
the alphabet is just too warm you up.

You get a rise out of me,
and I wanna speak in tongues,
and this is deeper than lust.
The way my heart beats
synthesizes the verbiage I leak,
with the embodiment of the feelings
that rush over me.

Damn,
you got that good, good from what I can see.
You trynna link?

Closed Mouths

You know closed mouths don't get fed?
So, you better crawl on them knees
and act like you want it.

I'm not asking you to beg or plead,
just give me what I need.

You know?
Hands up because,
these hands aren't doing any shooting.

They just trying to assist in the maneuvering.

foreplay can't be dead
with the illusions that fill my head!

See, I like it when you squirm!
Your eyes traveling down my spine,
fucking me at each and every curve.

Cause you see the visuals,
no misinterpretations
with this communication.

Closed Mouths

Summer Walker said,
"Women can't say when they want,
when they need or how!"
Well, shit I'm speaking.

I need it Monday thru friday
and even on the weekend;
cause these roles are reversed.

I control this Yoni-verse.
I'd love to grant you access,
when your words match your actions.

I'm not a role player,
I'm the whole team!

If you are thinking about choosing
well then, baby, I'm choosing me.

If you see me as the one,
then there's no need for another option.

Now back to what I said,
cause closed mouths don't get fed.

Closed Mouths

So, open up wide and enjoy
these slices of this warm, delicate pie.

And if you treat her good,
there's always a prize inside.

So, baby, don't hold back
express what's on your mind.

Good Wood

Smoking crack and blowing backs,
while laying this pipe like wood!
Split-her-enter only way I exit
is when I tweeze-her.

One-eighty on the head
to give her this wisdom.
funneled through gassing her up,
cause we're flowing tonight!

This back and forth is why
I only need one good pipe

A Taste

I'm trying to be your baby
and experience the entire world that is you,
via my mouth.

Dreamy

I enjoy looking at fine shit,
It makes me wonder,

How can I dip my
dreams in your gold.

The Motion

Kinesthetic pleasure,
imprints no measure,
movement gets it wetter.

Sensual F

I want you to be my sensual FUCK.
I wanna orgasm for every sense you light up.

Stimulate all of me,
and let me tell you,
there's more than 5 senses
when it comes to this body.

How Many Licks?

How many strokes does it take
to get the center of your tootsie to pop?

I'm trying to find out.

Is it one, two, or three?

Cause you know,
petite things can get into tight spaces.
But don't worry,
I'm trying to show you what these hips are all about.

Every thrust I've been working on in the gym,
I'm trying to put it to use.
This is my way of saying
if you throw it back, I'm gon' catch.

So, what you wanna do?

You can tell me, or we can find out.
I'm also cool with licking you like a lollipop,
until your tootsie falls out.

Addictive

a
Declaration
Determined
In
Circumstances
To
Insight
Vaginal
Eruptions.

Perfect Words

I found myself glancing through this book.
That seemed to have every word
that described you perfectly.
Dictionary, so thick
fitting my seams girthy.

How It Feels

Close your eyes and go there!!!
Do you remember how it feels?
How the silk glided;
How taste buds produced saliva;
How tension curled toes;
How the release seemed
to allow the body to float?
No gravity just faith and hope.
That even if the suspension broke
you'd know how to peak.
How to climax!
How to buckle at the knees.
Climbing above every cloud, eyes maxed.
Dreams worked, Paramounts of self-expression, so even
when all four walls were covered by shadows, you'd
remember how to get there even if you're eyes don't.
Illuminated in conviction,
A smile of ease,
A canvas painted
that doesn't require much thinking.
A Mona Lisa!
Close your eyes and go there.
The body always
remembers how it feels.

Do What You Do

There's nothing sexier
than watching you do what you love,
and it radiates through your effervescence.

It takes over how you postulate
every move in your style.
It makes my heart grow fonder,
and brings out my cheesy smile.

A true inspiration for me,
a reason as to why I still seek out my dreams.
I love watching you just
do what you do.

You, you a big boss to me.
I just love to watch you just be you.

Gruv

Baby, how can I GRUV you today?
Show you my gratitude, respect, understanding while
gaining your vulnerability?

Transparency looks sexy on you!
Take it all off and reveal to me
and only me how you move.

Wild and free, no restrictions
as we groove to our own
methodical beat.

structured around the values and principles
that makes it lovely to be naked
and in the wilderness.

Because oh so many times
do we lose our way.
Making it back to the path
Supported by our GRUV.

Honoring the mistakes that have been made into lessons,
kindled to wisdom;
and yet celebrating the smallest victories,

Gruv

because we still stand.
firmly planted in love.
fulfilled not just by our love, because
Sometimes love isn't enough.

But it's how we GRUV in this slow dance.
Tightly close moving as one,
a unit that can't be measured by worldly scales.
Mutually giving gratitude, respect, understanding, and
vulnerability.
Unrivaled in transparency.

Baby! How can I GRUV with you
for as long as we decide to stay?

Hot Potato

You ever pass a hot potato between two flames?
The flames get hotter, but never get burned.

The sizzle of the potato gets you excited for
when it's your turn.

Slow burns turning you on,
then all of a sudden you hear the background vocals
of that folded song.

Your fetishes be turning me on!
You can be my red light therapy
the way your wavelengths penetrate skin deep,
and release moans that even shock me.

Sizzle baby,
but don't run for this heat.
I invite you in this hot kitchen

Your Oyster

What you desire sitting inside of a shell.

When you split it open
can you take it in with one inhale;
Or do you like to play with your food?

An aphrodisiac that enhances the mood.
Tasting on your bud for that smooth,
tender, creamy, velvety mouthful.

Sweet and Juicy

Who left the faucet running?
Oh that's me every time I think about you.
I thought pineapples only made it sweet and juicy,
turns out she likes to get wet for you.

So, how wet do you want it?
How sweet is too sweet?
You know the blacker the berry the sweeter the juice,
the darker the flesh
you know it got some sweetness to it too.

I know it's hot outside,
do you need my juice?
Quench your thirst,
replenish your electrolytes,
Hydrate you,
get you prepared for boxing rounds,
cause this kitty knows how to fight.

Are you ready to drown in my love?
Well, come on and bust these pipes.
Have it Geysering like a New York City
fire hydrant on a 110 day back in 80's.

Sweet and Juicy

or you can have some fun like a slip n slide.
Either way this water parks for you,
just let me know when you to ride.
Apply some pressure to the bell in the center of my thighs.

Blank Canvas

Dip your body in them paints.
Apply your strokes to this canvas.
The art of war is what we paint.
Thin sheets can't stand us.
Cause they thread count don't add up.
If loving you was a mistake,
then I'm glad for the pieces that were shaped,
and the stains that will never fade away.
Because as they hang, they brighten up
a dull day.

Set The Pace

Since I got the time,
and I got the space.
Let me fill up your mind.

Will you go at my pace?
Love licking you down.
Put it all in my face.

Brace yourself with them sheets
when you scream out my name.
Don't say what you want do
when it's 50 shades of grey.

Intently placing kisses all over your waist.
Something so simple goes a long way.
Allow me to take the place of the pain.

Pleasuring your P is joy for me,
cause I wanna learn all the ways.
I just need your body.

New Heart Space

They say home is where's the hearts at,
well my hearts with you.
I thought I lost it but then
I found it when I made contact with you.

Experiencing an awaiting to exhale moment
and the feeling was new!
My bodies never had a chance to relax
and feel safe but when I'm with I do.

Calming my waters because they get chaotic
for these skies gloom,
and being so many's sunshine, my energy feels used.
So, when I meet you
I didn't know what to do!

Insured

Baby, I'll be your health insurance.
All you got to do is tell me where it hurt.
I'll play your doctor and your nurse.
I'll be your OB/GYN and your dental plan.
I don't know about psychology,
because I love it when you get crazy for me!
I'll rub your feet,
massage your back,
I'll do acupuncture if you needling all that!
Call me your body mechanic,
cause I'm trying to maintain all that!
Showing you that I see your value,
and I'm insuring all that!

Entry

I want one of them long clingy hugs
Cause I'm ready to flip some ish inside out!

More Than Physical

I love to hear you talk what you're passionate about,
we can have a nerds night out.

Talk your talk playa,
'lectoral notes are deep thoughts,
utilized as a cheat sheet, cause
if I know what brings you peace, I
ma be your peace freak.

Tongue lashing that makes you weak in the knees,
cause honestly, we don't need to speak.
Tantric union, just know you mean way more
than the physical to me

Right Place

Baby, let me tell you,
you are in the right place
at the right time!

Do you still believe in love?
Well, if not then
I'm here to give you mine.

No need to show and prove,
or compete for something
that enjoys spending time.

I'm not gon make it easy
for you to run and hide,
because you deserve love too.

That's why I want my fire
to spark what's on
you're inside

I wanna love you down
to your bare bone,
strip away, get naked for me,

Right Place

because with every strip I take
OUUU! you take my breath.
And I get to embrace
a new layer of you.

They told me
fairytales don't exist.
Well, I see my
fairytale with you.

When I wished upon a star
in the mist of my gloom,
I knew my dreams
were bound to come true.

Do you believe in love
as much as I do.
Well, then, baby

you are in the right place
at the right time.
Because the love that I
have is specially made for you.

Pin Up

Pinning things to the wall
must be one of your attributes,
because I'm not tall!
I stand below 5 foot 2.

But, this frame got a nice shape to it,
and enough weight for you
to make sure you hang on.

Don't drop this load, it's fragile,
and many have fumbled it,
passed it over for some worthlessness,
fool's gold,
bad investments,
but I think you know what you're holding.

White gloves
and soft strokes
keep that diamond glowing.

Mirror

What do I see when I see you?
I'm glad you asked.
I see me,
a passionate lover;
that's been heartbroken by many.
Hiding out
while trying to put the pieces back together.
finding peace in solitude
while still longing to love another.
See, I might be good with my words now,
but not that long ago I couldn't tell you how.
Questioning what love is
because it's ruled in my life with heavy hands, hidden
intentions, and crooked smile after smile.
Constantly giving,
hoping that it would give in,
until I found myself overly giving.
Losing myself in the process.
Diminishing God's initial mission.
To be free!
To love unconditionally with his heart.
Understanding that all is not forgotten or lost,
even when you have to spread apart,

Mirror

separate, go your different ways.
Wanting to change, but still clinching
on to what no longer serves us.
You are the yin to my yang.
If I am the sun, then you are my moon!
forcing you to love me is something I want do.
I release you with love, so that you can bloom,
because if I'm looking in the mirror,
that's what I'd want me to do.
I see the tears in your eyes, and it's okay to let them run.
When you do, just know the journey of healing,
and loving you has only begun.
I stand here planted, ready and willing to embrace you
when all the work is done.
Because when I see you,
I see me,
longing for the same passionate love.

50/50 Where?

Baby,
I don't know what 50/50 is,
I'm bringing 100% of what I got to the table,
we like Vin diagrams,
two wholes just crossing paths,
not just made to compare and contrast,
but to analyze our strengths and weaknesses.
Where you are strong, and I am weak,
gives way for you to teach;
and lessons gon' always come when wisdom speaks.
Love has never been easy,
but the choice to love you seemed meek.

Summertime

It's summer, summer, summertime!
And oh my!
Are you summertime fine!
That outside in,
I mean that inside out.
Them flowie, floral printed,
waist indented,
what I'd like to start my next paragraph about.

Just draping along
your curvaceous spout.
Those Appalachian roads,
you know where only
one car gets to pass go.

Your cliff hanger!
While you sachet on by
ripened with an eccentrically, enticing,
electrified vibe.
Oooh!
You smirking.

Summertime

Cause you knowing what you
possess in your trunk.
Enough to make the smallest
passersby's pacifier get stuck.

Can I have you on that TLC tip?
Your body as a charcuterie board
and my next picnic?

Normal I'm not outside,
but since trends keep on circling the block,
I'm in my Tupac bag.
Trynna get around,
around something sleazy
to tease me,
that can squeeze me,
but takes it nice and easy.

Cause it's the summertime,
and while the formations
keep on formulating,
how I'm making this Lemonade.
I'm trynna keep myself together

Summertime

like Bey' and Jay.

Oh yeah!
How you make me smile.
The strut of your walk,
the sway in them hips!

You the summertime
I'm trynna get outside
to pinch hit.

This is it!
No this is us!
Summer Lover Pervusing
all in that sundress.

Close to Her

This is the best time of year,
to get up close to her
and whisper something with flavor in her ear!

Let her know how much you want to be up under her,
inhaling her sweet nectar
every time she tells you to come hear.

Silent moans grow louder
making symphonies with rain drops
and furnace heat.

What an aroma all this might be,
filling rooms like Thanksgiving Turkey.

finger licking her good
as she comes from the home state of
The Kentucky Derby.

Sugar

Yeah, you sweet!
I like how your sugar canes
white meat is buried under a tough exterior,
because with this machete I keep on cutting.
Whips to my back,
blisters on my fingertips,
arms heavier than cruise ships,
knees weak like I'm Boyz to Men.
But I don't tire easily.
The shimmer of that pearl energizes me.
Solar panels that's eco-friendly.
No need to replace these batteries,
Rose is a name that runs deeply in my ancestry.
You, a puzzle I don't wanna figure out!
I enjoy the challenge
of the many ways I can spread you out,
mix you in,
Betty cooker my world,
Aunt Jemima's my girl,
but it's you I really want.
A juice until it dries,
and leaves behind a crack-like residue.

Sugar

Damn! I think I'm hooked on you
You sweet!
Sweeter than a honey bunny.
Come on and glaze my heart,
cause it needs your sweet loving.

Sweet Tooth

You know I talk about sweets a lot
cause I got a sweet tooth,
and I've been sizing you up;
cause I wanna taste the sweetest parts of you.

Thicker than a snicker!
If you melt in my hand
and not in my mouth
I want be made.

I'd lick her.
Although, I actually like to reverse that,
because a Hershey's kiss
is where I want my mouth.

On Me!

ON me!
ON me!
Like O-N me.

A spread.
Be the peanut butter to my jelly.
Thick, smooth, maybe a crunch
here and there to keep things
a little exciting.

Do you like yo' jelly with flavor
or maybe you'd like
her honey or nut-tel-la?

But there's nothing like that classic.
Still thick, sticky, moist, with a little shake
and she still remains posed.

OWN me!

I give you permission.
Like O-W-N me!
When we get into that

On Me!

mission-airy position.

Like, put these legs in a V
while you get in between.
Make this jelly shake
because there's no jam!

Stamina remains high
the way you spread.
Ouu got damn!

Your peanut butter,
with my jelly!
Is always a W.
No matter the spelling,
as long as it's ON me.

And, since you got the spread,
then I got the cream.

Playtime

Me!

Play with the pussy?
HELL NAW, I'm trynna stay in it!

She the gusher I need
getting stuck in my teeth.

Now or later, I'm always sucking.

Turn Yourself On

Can you turn yourself on
to the point where you almost climax?
Please, show me all the ways!
I am a student ready for you to be my teacher.

Give me all the details or
you can leave it open,
and I'll fill in all the blanks,
with each of your moans.

But, it's such a turn on
to know that you know how you like it.
Talk to me, Coach me through it.
I love the sound of your voice
when you take control,

never demanding
it's like you're talking sensual.

My ears perk up,
my gaze goes soft,
and before you know it
I could be drooling down south.

Turn Yourself On

It is a pleasure to please you,
because you know you better than I do.
I'm just trying to get my
hands on that blueprint.
Just to make mistakes,
so you can correct me!

Guide me,
I wanna see it your way,
as a matter of fact, go on
and stand behind me.

Rose Petaled

That rose petal love,
Soft skin every time we touch, ugh!
The layers of you.

HOLIDAY SOECIAL

Come here,
can I whisper something in your ear?
I'm not a gift but
I'd like to be unwrapped by you!
We can be naughty and nice
saving old Saint Nick a trip for the night.
Because, My favorite time of year is now!
Setting out my freshly baked cookies and some warm milk
to wash it all down.
Making sure my chimney
is cleared so my Santa can find his way.
No need to leave me a present
under the tree as long as I can ride his sleigh. Crossing
every time zone in one complete day.
And by the end of the night
everything leads back to the North Pole.
And depending on the angle
it could be heading down south.
Roasting every chestnut along the way.
Even frosty likes my melt down.
Jingling your bells all through town.
Hitting notes that Carey's peak
because all I want for Christmas is you.

HOLIDAY SOECIAL

No Mariah (mirage) of the science type because
Ai has nothing
on this cinnamon clove.
How do you think Rudolph
has such a bright nose?
Evergreens and peppermints;
cedar and gingerbread
but trust you don't have to catch me.
The muffin man knows how to kneed
out his dough.
And if you're rolling them hips
This Christmas, like Chris Brown
even frozen rivers will flow.
If you gotta put coal in my stocking
for being naughty tonight,
just make sure it's of the diamond type,
cause adding force to this load
is going to make your heart grow
three times its size,
and have you flying
seeing northern lights
while bellowing out HO HO HO!
So, come here!
Let me whisper something in your ear.

CREAM

Strawberries with cream,
my tongue for milking your way,
a delightful taste.

SAY YES

The sexiest thing a lover could ever tell me is YES!
How the ye- sounds with the sizzle of a drawn out Sssss!
It's the year of the snake so I follow the path that leads to sacredness.

I'm connected with you in more than one way,
because to say yes is to surrender.
That's permission, a Godly intervention.

Can I whisper in your ear? (Yes)
Can I twirl my fingers in your hair? (Yes)
Can I kiss you soft starting at your temples and end up everywhere? (Yes)

Don't fret if the answers No,
I can take it slow.
I can be here for a while cause I love it when you smile.
It's all in the experience for me.

Can I hold you close and breathe in your energy? (Yes)
Can I frustrate you a little, so we can look intently in each other's eyes? (Yes)
Can I fill you up with my words and let my actions follow? (Yes)

SAY YES

You can be the Lyrics of my verse
because the way you got me feeling
I can be serial in these sheets.
Mmm, your vibrational tones remind me of honey bees.

And you wanna know what's funny to me? (Yes)

How everybody gets excited for Valentine's Day,
cause for me, I need more than one day to express my love.
I need forever!

So you know whatchu gotta say?

All you got to do is say yes!
Don't deny what you feel,
let me undress you, babe
Open up your mind and just rest
I'm about to let you know, you make me so

JONEZ N

I just wanna fill you up with my words cause you the shit
girl, is that alright?

I see you girl!
A taste of splendor in this rainbow world!
How your hair drapes over your shoulders,
wanting to be a part of your frame
to take sips of that Coca-Cola.

So, I wonder if I place this mentos against your soft walls
will you explode?

You the blues to my Nina
I am just trying to hear Simone.
My hands are like magnets
and your body has this gravitational pull.

It's like forbidden fruit.
I'm only human
trying to satisfy the summer eve in me,
so let's rough ride.

And it's like every time we talk
with every word you speak it sounds like a moan,

JONEZ N

damn can you kiss me through the phone?

I'm Jones'N for you!
I got a bit of blues in that left
and some funk in that right,
add a little spin to it we can
Tamia shuffle all night.

Cause I can't get enough of you girl!
You made splash in this world
that capsized every fantasy.
And every wild dream
I just envision you and me.

Like you're face against that wall
and my hands riding up your thighs,
while whispers fill your ears
pull them panties to the side.
I got 5 fingers, can you make 2 disappear?

Yeah,
I see you biting your lips
thinking about how that might feel.

JONEZ N

Ain't no situation-ships this is a Love Jones.
You my something, something
and I'm trying to break you off.

I don't just mean sexual.
Our intimacy is deepen when you not next me.
I feel us growing in congruency

When you walk away it has a pull on me,
cause you're the sweetest thing I've known.
I'm just trying to place my kisses on your collarbone,
fingertips caressing your skin,
affirmatively fucking you,
reassuring you that there's nothing like this Love Jones.

Black Love reimagined,
even the bullshit can't divide us,
because even if we do split
we find our way back home.

Pictures say a thousand words,
while these poems paint pictures!
I see you vividly, girl!
Can I add you to this elixir?

JONEZ N

I'm Jones'N for you!
So, come on and let me
show you what this
Love Jones can do.

A Darius with his Nina
jazzing to some Simone.
Is that alright?

DEFINITION OF INTIMACY

in·ti·ma·cy
/ˈin(t)əməsē/

noun

close familiarity or friendship; closeness.
"the intimacy between a husband and wife"

Similar:
closeness, togetherness, affinity, rapport, attachment, familiarity, confidentiality, close association, close relationship, close attachment, close friendship, friendliness, comradeship, companionship, amity, affection, mutual affection, warmth, warm feelings. understanding, fellow feeling, chumminess, palliness, mateyness

a private, cozy atmosphere.
"the room had a peaceful sense of intimacy about it"
euphemistic
an intimate act, especially sexual intercourse.

www.ingramcontent.com/pod-product-compliance
Lightning Source LLC
LaVergne TN
LVHW090618110826
845146LV00001B/435

* 9 7 9 8 9 9 5 1 4 5 6 0 8 *